Chinese Modern Engineering

HIGH-SPEED RAIL

Edited by Xia Rui   Written by Yu Liyuan   Illustrated by Wang Futing

Books Beyond Boundaries

ROYAL COLLINS

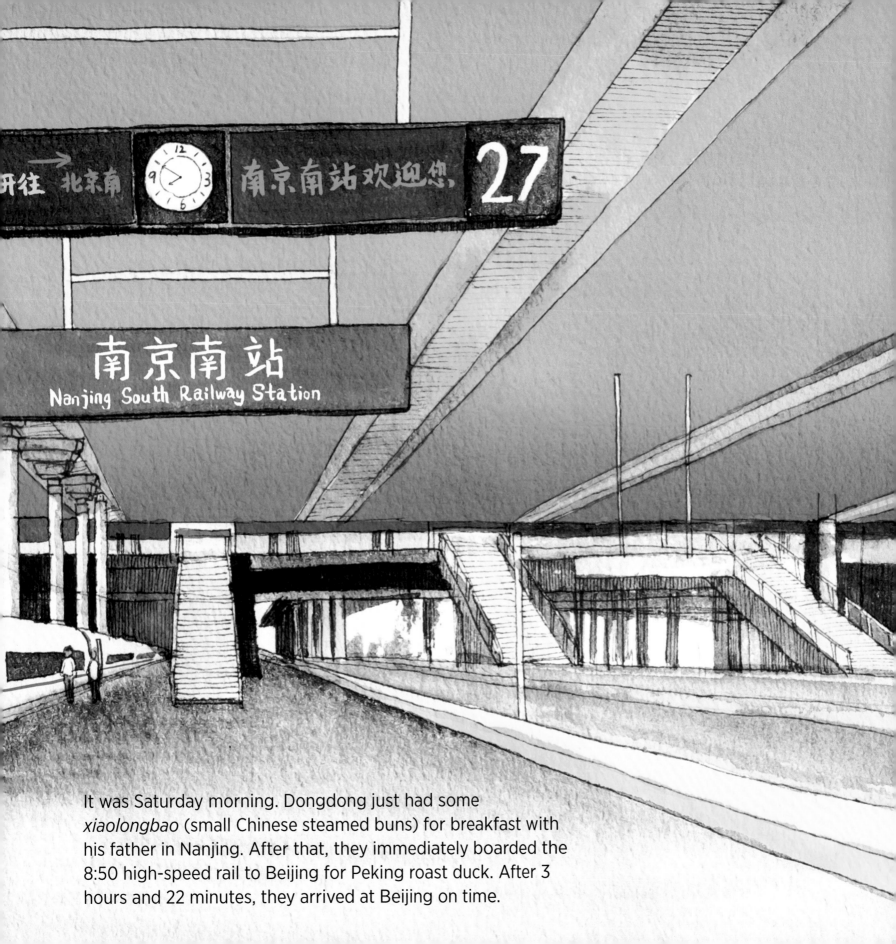

It was Saturday morning. Dongdong just had some *xiaolongbao* (small Chinese steamed buns) for breakfast with his father in Nanjing. After that, they immediately boarded the 8:50 high-speed rail to Beijing for Peking roast duck. After 3 hours and 22 minutes, they arrived at Beijing on time.

His father told him how travelling was much more difficult in ancient times. At first, people could only **walk wherever they wanted to go**. If someone walked 40 km per day, it would take him more than 30 days to go from Nanjing to Beijing.

Sometime later, people learned to domesticate animals through hunting. People didn't have to walk on their own anymore when **oxen and horses were trained to carry them**.

However, horseback riding required specific techniques. In addition, horses couldn't carry a lot of goods on their backs. Therefore, people invented carriages that could carry both people and cargo.

Soon, people found out that **carriages** moved faster along early wheel traces. So they paved trails for carriages. A **horsecar** (horse-drawn railway) could carry more passengers and more cargo.

Railway originated from horsecar trails.

In 1825, the world's first modern railway was opened between Stockton and Darlington in England. The steam locomotive *Voyager* was successfully tested on this railroad. But people didn't fall in love with the slow engine right away.

In 1829, after the railroad from Liverpool to Manchester was completed, a special contest was held between steam locomotives and carriages to decide which was better. At last, Robert Stephenson's *Rocket* won. From that time, steam locomotives began to gradually replace horsecars.

In some regions where coal is scarce and difficult to get from elsewhere, people use firewood to replace coal as fuel.

Steam locomotives are fed on coal, meaning they burn coal to turn water into steam to provide power. Because coal burning produces flames, Chinese people call steam locomotives "fire cars" (**trains**).

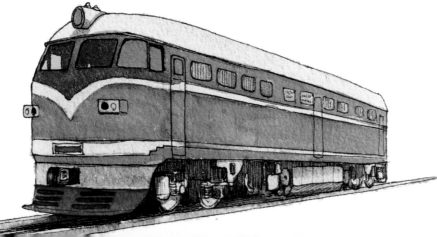

However, people realized that steam locomotives need to stop frequently at the stations to add coal and water; what's more, the black smoke harms the environment as well as people's health. So, a new train that feeds on fuel oil—**the diesel locomotive**—was invented.

Diesel locomotives are not only faster but also more environmentally-friendly.

When trains used electric power, **the electric locomotive** was born. This type of train does not burn coal or oil and has zero pollution. It is fast and powerful.

The electric locomotive is not self-powered. It runs on external electricity.

With the continuous development of railway technology, we are now in the age of **high-speed rail**.

In 1964, on the eve of the Tokyo Olympic Games, Tokaido Shinkansen between Tokyo and Osaka was officially open. The "0 series" trains were the fastest in the world, and ran at a speed of 200 km per hour.

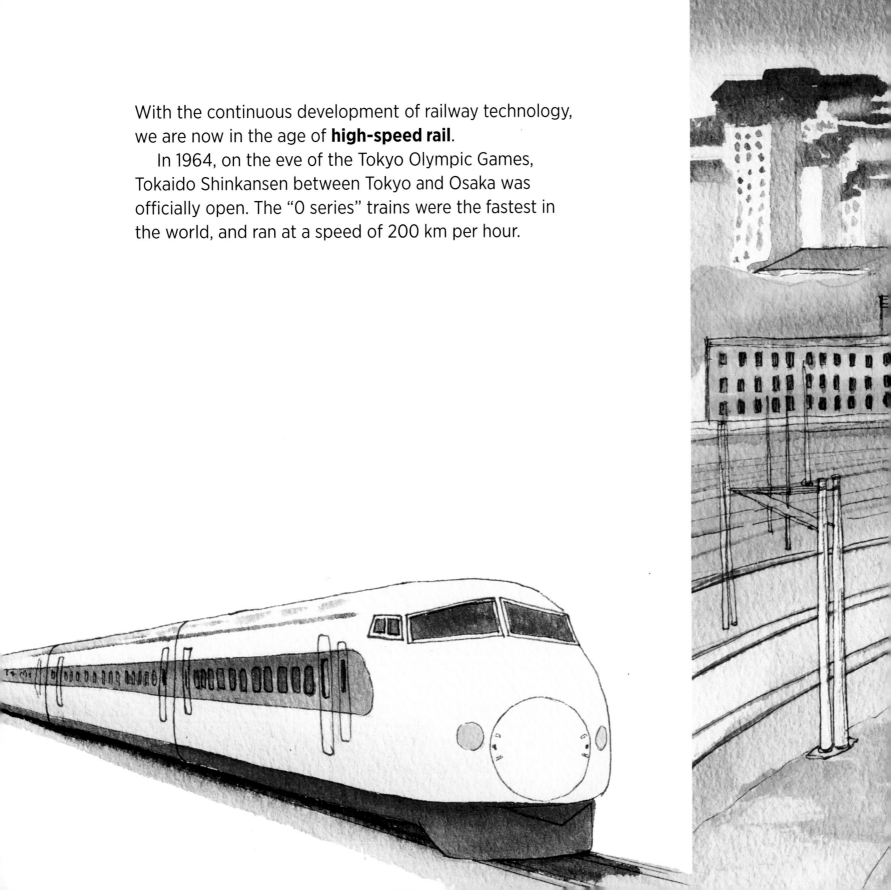

On August 1, 2008, one week before Beijing Olympic Games, China's first high-speed rail—the Beijing-Tianjin intercity railway opened. The maximum speed of **Hexie CRH trains** could reach 350 km per hour.

What makes high-speed rail capable of reaching such a high speed?

It's their super power.

The carriages of regular trains do not have the power of their own and can only be dragged by the locomotive. When the train starts, the locomotive needs to drag the first carriage, and then it drags the second carriage with the first carriage . . . this is a lot of work for the locomotive.

High-speed rail, on the other hand, is a multiple-unit train. These are self-propelled carriages combined with carriages that need to be dragged along. When the train starts, the self-propelled carriages will operate at the same time to push the whole train forward. This, of course, is a lot faster than single powered trains.

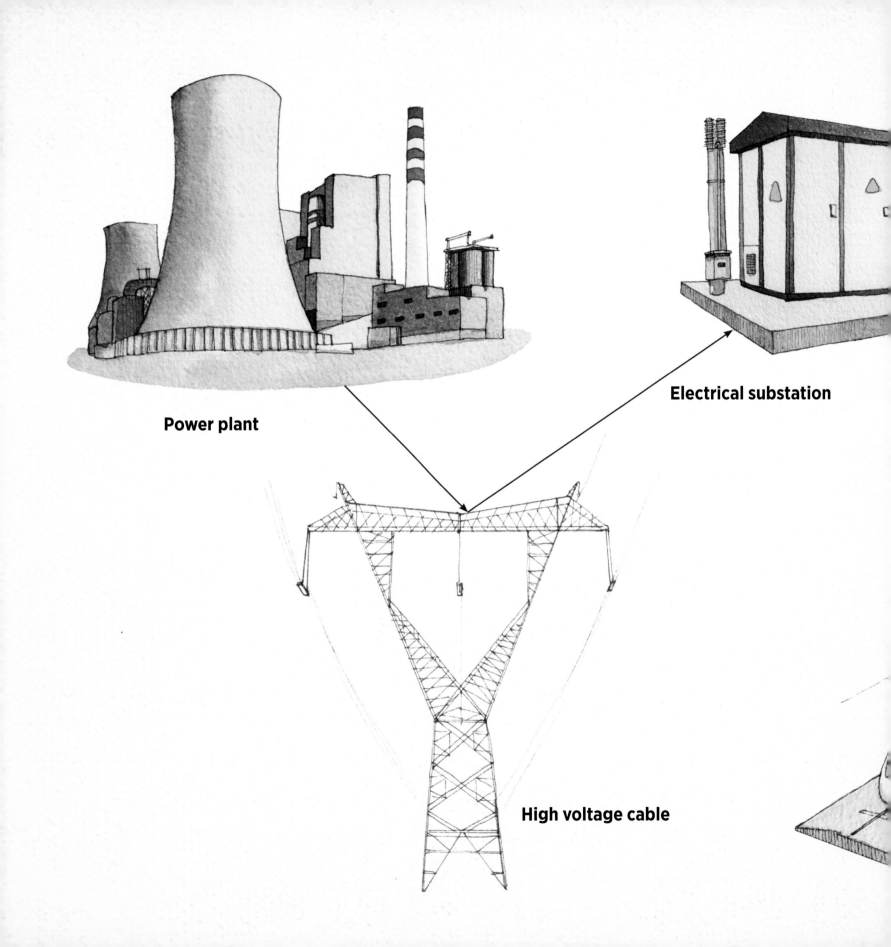

Power plant

Electrical substation

High voltage cable

The high-speed rail is propelled by electricity. It has a complete electrical supply system. The wire-like device above the train is the catenary. It covers all high-speed railways and provides power for running trains at all times and places.

Catenary and pantograph

The pantograph receives electricity from the catenary and transmits it to self-propelled trains.

Transformer station

The transformer station receives electricity from the power plant, converts it into electricity suitable for high-speed trains, and then transmits it to the catenary.

Trains and railway

At last, electricity will return to the substation through the railway.

In the past, when the steam trains traveled on regular railways, they made loud banging noises. This was the sound of wheels running over the places where the tracks were connected.

The railway track is made of welded segments, usually several tens of meters long. Trains will shake when they drive over these connections, and passengers will feel shaky as well.

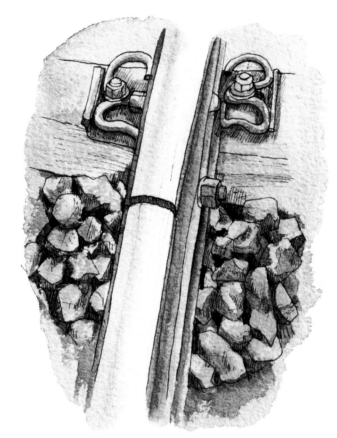

When trains are going at a high speed, the interfaces like this can make the trains derail. It is very dangerous. Therefore, high-speed railways are seamless rails.

The seamless rails are segmented when they are first produced. They will need to be welded to the length of about 1,640 feet in factories and then transported to the laying site. There, they will be welded again into several hundred kilometers of seamless rails, so high-speed trains will not shake at all when running on it.

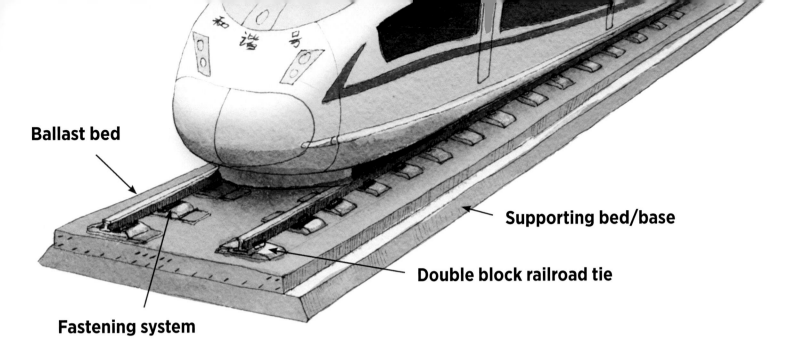

Ballast bed

Fastening system

Supporting bed/base

Double block railroad tie

Double block ballast-less track

Another crucial element that enables fast and smooth driving of high-speed rail is ballast-less track.

Ballast refers to the rubble used to make the ballast bed below the railroad ties and the track for traditional railways. This rubble can make the track more elastic and disperse the pressure of the train.

III style fastener

Ballast bed

However, if the speed of the train is too high, splattering rubble will cause damage to the train and affect its safety. Therefore, China's high-speed railways generally apply ballast-less tracks. They are more sustainable and safer for the trains.

Steel track

Railroad tie

High-speed rail has a high demand for a smooth and straight route. Each seamless rail is more than 1,640 feet long and cannot be turned. So bridges or tunnels need to be built to ensure the high-speed rail goes straight.

Have you noticed that the tunnel openings of high-speed rail are generally in the shape of a trumpet? This is because when the train goes through the tunnel at high speed, the air will be squeezed and cause pain to our eardrums. The trumpet-shaped tunnel opening will reduce the pressure on our ears.

High-speed railroad needs to adapt to all kinds of terrains in order to reach more places.

For example, there is a type of soil with ice in it, called frozen soil. It is very hard in cold weather.

However, if the temperature rises, the frozen soil will soften and even collapse.

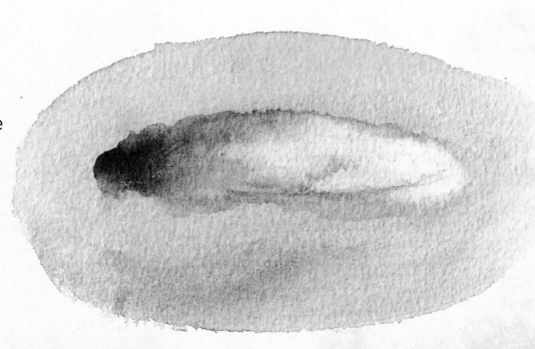

To address this problem, engineers use metal bars to bring underground heat into the air so that the temperature of the frozen soil remains low.

High-speed rail bridges have deep piers. The roadbed is little affected by the frozen soil, and trains can run safely on it.

With the financial support from the government and the hard work of engineers, China's high-speed rail construction has achieved great success in recent years.

By the end of 2020, the operating mileage of China's high-speed railway reached 37,900 km, which was the longest in the world.

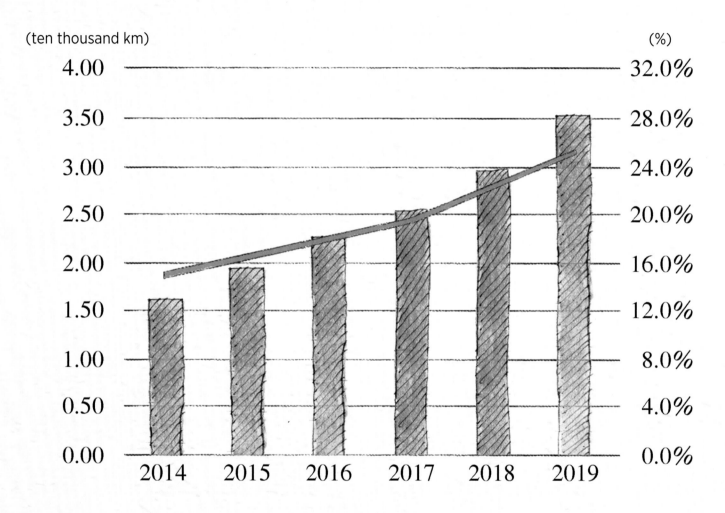

Operating mileage and proportion of high-speed rail

operating mileage (ten thousand km)   proportion in railway operating mileage (%)

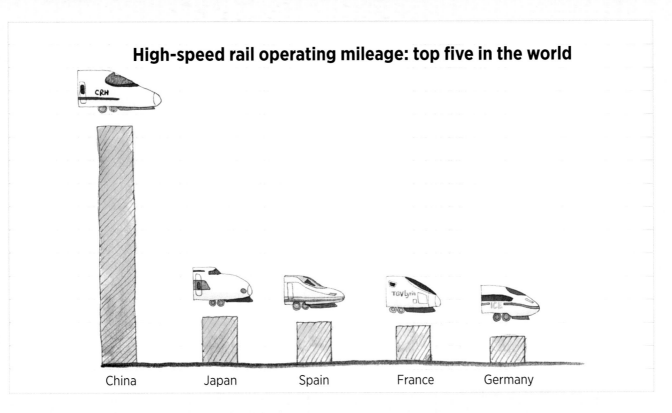

High-speed rail operating mileage: top five in the world

The development of China's high-speed railway has been leading in the world. It is now a shiny new brand of the country.

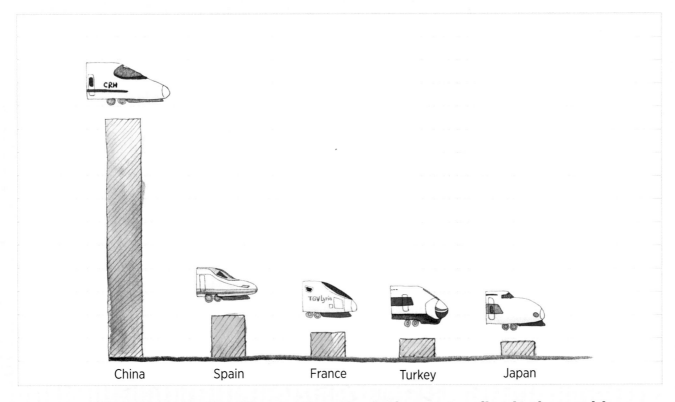

High-speed rail under construction mileage: top five in the world

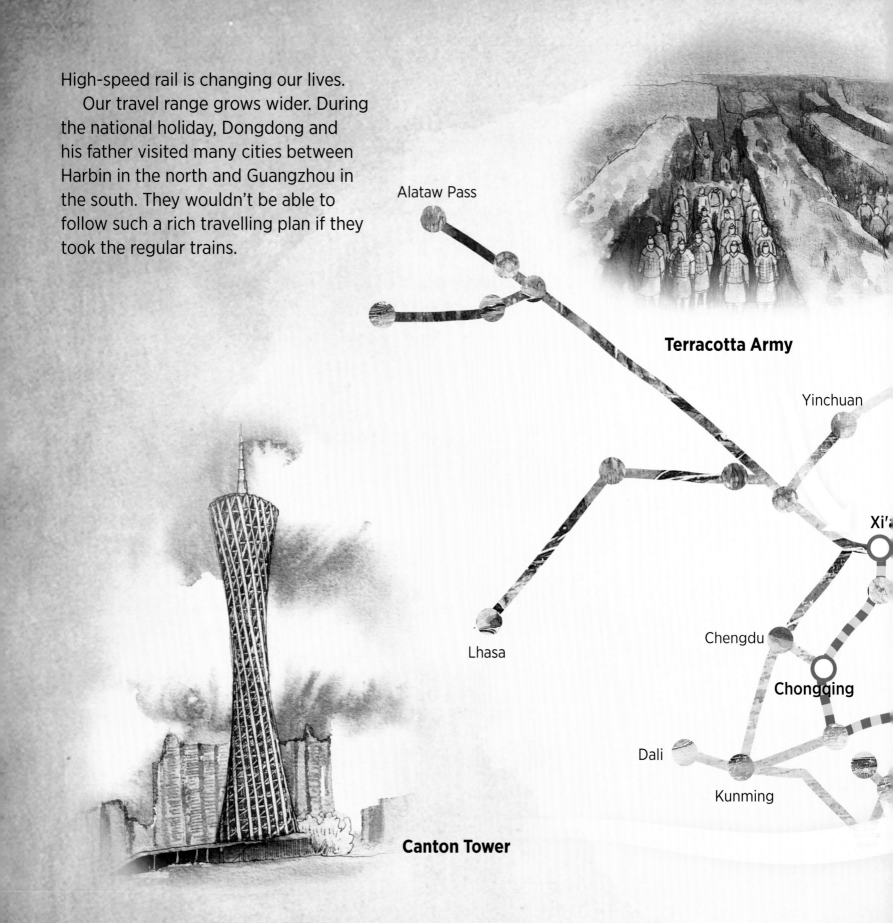

High-speed rail is changing our lives.

Our travel range grows wider. During the national holiday, Dongdong and his father visited many cities between Harbin in the north and Guangzhou in the south. They wouldn't be able to follow such a rich travelling plan if they took the regular trains.

Alataw Pass

Terracotta Army

Yinchuan

Xi'a

Chengdu

Lhasa

Chongqing

Dali

Canton Tower

Kunming

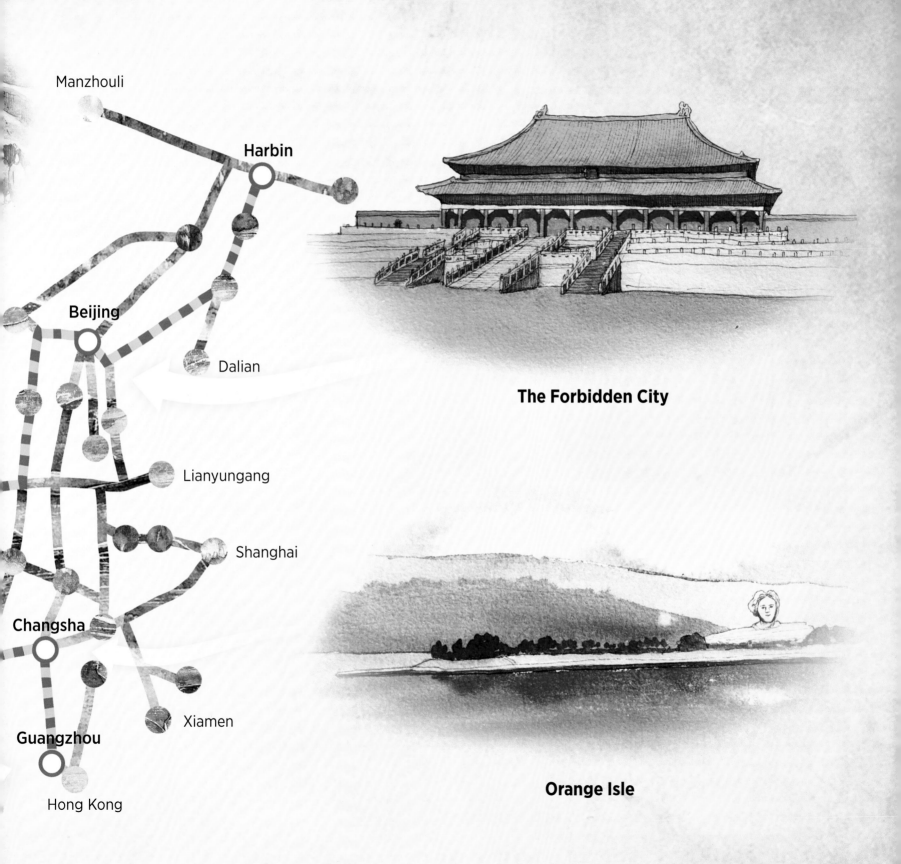

Manzhouli

Harbin

Beijing

Dalian

Lianyungang

Shanghai

Changsha

Xiamen

Guangzhou

Hong Kong

The Forbidden City

Orange Isle

The high-speed rail makes the distance between cities shorter and brings people closer.

In the past, it was always difficult to buy train tickets on holidays. Many people working away from home were not able to spend Spring Festival with their families. For people who were lucky to get a ticket, they would still need to endure a long, crowded, and noisy journey back home.

The high-speed rail solved the biggest transportation problem in China—the Spring Festival travel rush. Train tickets are no longer hard to get, and people living and working in different cities can also return home more frequently. The comfortable seats on high-speed trains also make their journey more enjoyable.

"I am ripe!"

"The high-speed rail will take us to big cities."

The high-speed rail also improves the speed of logistics.

"On hot summer days, mom will buy lychee online. They are shipped by high-speed trains from Putian and will arrive in Beijing on the same day."

"I am still fresh!"

Fuling

Xuanhan

Pingchang County

Wanyuan City

Tongjiang County

Ziwu Town

Chang'an

In the old days, it was not so easy for people in the north to taste fresh fruit from the south.

The famous beauty Empress Yang Guifei in the 8th century loved lychees. There were no lychees in Chang'an, so they had to be brought to her from the nearest lychee fields. Several delivery men would take turns carrying the lychee on horseback, and they had to ride day and night without stopping. In spite of this, it would take three to four days before the last delivery man could arrive at the capital. What a great price it took for people in the past to eat lychees!

In areas where high-speed rail is open, people's travel is not limited by distance. The local economic development is also greatly benefited. Nevertheless, due to various reasons, there are still many places where high-speed rail hasn't reached. But one day, the high-speed rail network will cover these regions as well and make more people's lives easier and happier.

At present, the operating speed of China's high-speed trains is 200–350 km per hour. In the future, it is said that there will be a "super high-speed train" that can go faster than 1,000 km per hour! This super train will be built with vacuum pipeline and magnetic levitation technology, which will even make it go faster than regular planes!

Some people also say that in the future, high-speed trains will not need to stop at stations, but passengers can still board and get off the train. **What do you think the future trains will be like?**

ABOUT THE EDITOR:

Xia Rui is the general manager of the Jiangsu Qiaomu Education Technology Co., Ltd. He graduated from the Department of Chemistry in the National University of Singapore, and then started teaching Cambridge and Oxford University Entrance courses in the International Department of the Nanjing Foreign Languages School. He is proficient in English, physics, chemistry, mathematics, and other disciplines. He has written and directed many books, such as *Exam Key Points Analysis*, *Calculation Expert*, and *Preparatory Courses*, which are considered first-line brands in the market.

ABOUT THE ILLUSTRATOR:

Wang Futing graduated from the School of Animation in the China Academy of Art. Her graduation works have won the Silver Award in the Taiwan Creative Design Competition, the Bronze Award of the Kunshan Animation Fest, and the Finalist Award of China International Animation Fest. Ever since her graduation, Wang has worked as a professional illustrator for picture books and commercials. She participated in the R&D and illustration project for the *Modern Engineering* picture book series.

CHINESE MODERN ENGINEERING:
HIGH-SPEED RAIL

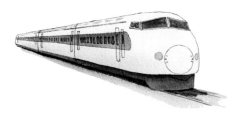

Edited by Xia Rui
Written by Yu Liyuan
Illustrated by Wang Futing

First published in 2022 by Royal Collins Publishing Group Inc.
Groupe Publication Royal Collins Inc.
BKM Royalcollins Publishers Private Limited

Headquarters: 550-555 boul. René-Lévesque O Montréal (Québec) H2Z1B1 Canada
India office: 805 Hemkunt House, 8th Floor, Rajendra Place, New Delhi 110 008

Original Edition © Hohai University Press

ISBN: 978-1-4878-0943-0

To find out more about our publications, please visit www.royalcollins.com.